THE ROMAN EMPIRE

*What life was like in the
ancient world*

Philip Steele

Consultant: Jenny Hall, Museum of London

southwater

This edition published by Southwater

Distributed in the UK by
The Manning Partnership
251-253 London Road East, Batheaston
Bath BA1 7RL
UK
tel. (0044) 01225 852 727
fax. (0044) 01225 852 852

Distributed in the USA by
Ottenheimer Publishing
5 Park Center Court
Suite 300
Owing Mills MD 2117-5001
USA
tel. (001) 410 902 9100
fax. (001) 410 902 7210

Distributed in Australia by
Sandstone Publishing
Unit 1, 360 Norton Street
Leichhardt
New South Wales 2040
Australia
tel. (0061) 2 9560 7888
fax. (0061) 2 9560 7488

Distributed in New Zealand
by
Five Mile Press NZ
PO Box 33-1071
Takapuna, Auckland 9
New Zealand
tel. (0064) 9 486 1925
fax. (0064) 9 486 1454

Southwater is an imprint of Anness Publishing Limited
© 1997, 2000 Anness Publishing Limited

1 3 5 7 9 10 8 6 4 2

Publisher: Joanna Lorenz
Managing Editor: Sue Grabham
Senior Editor: Ambreen Husain
Editor: Charlotte Evans
Designer: John Jamieson
Illustration: Stuart Carter
Photography: John Freeman
Stylist: Thomasina Smith

Anness Publishing would like to thank the following
children for modelling for this book: Mohammed Asfar,
Leon R. Banton, Afsana Begum, Ha Chu, Paula Dent,
Frankie Timothy Junior Elliot, Rikky Charles Healey,
Eva Rivera/Razbadavskite, Simon Thexton,
Shereen Thomas and Ha Vinh.

CONTENTS

PICTURE CREDITS
b=bottom, t=top, c=centre, l=left, r=right
Lesley and Roy Adkins Picture Library: pages 5cr, 13t, 31bl,
35b, 38l, 39b and 55tl; Ancient Art and Architecture
Collection Ltd: pages 8b, 8l, 9tl, 9tc, 11tl, 14b, 21tr, 21cl,
21cr, 24/25, 27r, 31bl, 32b, 33tl, 33br, 36, 41t, 42b, 49tr,
50bl, 52tr, 52bl, 54tr, 57tl, 61bl; A-Z Botanical Collection
Ltd: page 53br; The Bridgeman Art Library: page 13b; The
British Museum: pages 22r, 23tr, 23cr, 23bl, 28c, 28r, 30l, 42c,
48bl, 48br, 49b, 52br, 57b and 63bc; Peter Clayton: pages 18l,
25cr, 34tl and 37bc; C M Dixon: pages 10l, 12bl, 14t, 15bl,

17tl, 17cr, 20bl, 24bl, 25tr, 25br, 26l, 26r, 27l, 29tl, 29tc, 29tr, 30
32/33, 33bl, 34tr, 34b, 35t, 35c, 37tl, 37tr, 38br, 40cl, 40tr, 41bl,
45tl, 45cl, 45bl, 47t, 47c, 48tr, 49tl, 50tl, 50br, 51tl, 55tr, 55b, 56
57tr, 58tr, 58bl, 58br, 60l, 60r, 62t, 63c, title page, front cover and
cover; Geoscience Features Picture Library: page 61tr; Sonia Hallida
Photographs: pages 15tl, 38tr and 63tl; Michael Holford Photograph
pages 3t, 5tr, 12tr, 12br, 16, 22l, 28l, 29br, 37bl, 40bl, 40br, 45br
46bl, 51tr, 51bl, 53bl, 54bl, 61tl and 62br; Simon James: pages 43
and 43br; Mary Evans Picture Library: pages 9bl, 9br, 10r, 20tr, 29
44b, 54br, 56r and 59r; Planet Earth Pictures Ltd: page 5b; Tony S
Images: pages 4/5; Visual Arts Library: pages 39tr and 46/47; Werr
Forman Archive: pages 21bl and 53t; Zefa: pages 8r, 15br and 47b.

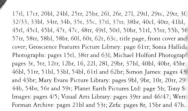

The Story of Rome

THE CITY OF ROME today is a bustling place, full of traffic and crowds. But if you could travel back in time to 800BC, you would find only a few small villages on peaceful, wooded hillsides along the banks of the river Tiber. According to legend, Rome was founded here in 753BC. In the centuries that followed, the Romans came to dominate Italy and the Mediterranean. They farmed and traded and fought for new lands. Rome grew to become the center of a vast empire that stretched across Europe into Africa and Asia. The Roman Empire brought a sophisticated way of life to vast numbers of people. Many Roman buildings and artifacts still survive and help show us what life was like in the time of the Roman Empire.

ROMAN ITALY
As the city of Rome prospered, the Romans gradually conquered neighboring tribes. By 250BC they controlled most of Italy. This map shows some of the important towns and cities of that time.

ANCIENT AND MODERN
In Rome today, people live alongside the temples, marketplaces and public buildings of the past. This is the Colosseum, a huge arena called an amphitheater. It was used for staging games and fights, and first opened to the public in AD80.

TIMELINE 753BC–276BC

Rome's rise to power was sudden and spectacular. Its eventful history includes bloody battles, eccentric emperors, amazing inventions and remarkable feats of engineering. The Roman Empire prospered for almost 500 years, and still influences the way we live today.

Romulus, the first king of Rome

c. 753BC The city of Rome is founded by Romulus, according to legend.

673–641BC Tullus Hostilius, Rome's third king, expands the city's territory by conquering a neighboring settlement. Rome's population doubles as a result.

641–616BC Pons Sublicius, the first bridge across the river Tiber, is constructed.

The harbor town of Ostia is founded at the mouth of the Tiber.

600BC The Latin language is first written in a script that is still used today.

inscription in Latin, carved in stone

750BC   700BC   650BC   600BC

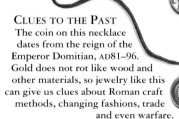

CLUES TO THE PAST
The coin on this necklace dates from the reign of the Emperor Domitian, AD81–96. Gold does not rot like wood and other materials, so jewelry like this can give us clues about Roman craft methods, changing fashions, trade and even warfare.

ARCHAEOLOGISTS AT WORK
These archaeologists are excavating sections of wallplaster from the site of a Roman house in Britain. Many remains of Roman buildings and artifacts, as well as books and documents, have survived over the years. These all help us build up a picture of what life was like in the Roman Empire.

SECRETS BENEATH THE SEA
Divers have discovered Roman shipwrecks deep under the waters of the Mediterranean Sea. Many have their cargo still intact. These jars were being transported over 2,000 years ago. By examining shipwrecks, archaeologists can learn how Roman boats were built, what they carried and where they traded.

Jupiter, one of the most important Roman gods

493BC The office of Tribune is created to protect the rights of the plebeians, the common people.

509BC The Temple of Jupiter in Rome is completed.

Rome becomes a republic, throwing out the last king.

Servius Tullius, the king after whom the Servian Wall was named

Celtic warrior

390BC Celtic warriors ransack Rome.

380BC The Servian Wall is built to defend Rome from any future attacks.

312BC The construction of the Via Appia, Rome's first great road, begins.

The Aqua Appia, Rome's first aqueduct, is built.

an aqueduct

| 550BC | 500BC | 450BC | 400BC | 350BC | 300BC |

The Great Empire

BY THE YEAR AD117, the Roman Empire was at its apex. It was possible to travel 2,480 miles from east to west and still hear the trumpets of the Roman legions. As a Roman soldier you might have had to shiver in the snowy winters of northern Britain, or sweat and toil in the heat of the Egyptian desert.

The peoples of the Empire were very different. There were Greeks, Egyptians, Syrians, Jews, Africans, Germans and Celts. Many of them belonged to civilizations that were already ancient when Rome was still a group of villages. Many revolted against Roman rule, but uprisings were quickly put down. Gradually, conquered peoples came to accept being part of the Empire. From AD212 onward, any free person living under Roman rule had the right to claim "I am a Roman citizen." Slaves, however, had very few rights.

In AD284, after a series of violent civil wars, this vast empire was divided into several parts. Despite being reunited by the Emperor Constantine in AD324, the Empire was doomed. A hundred years later, the western part was invaded by fierce warriors from the north, with disastrous consequences. Although the Western Empire came to an end in AD476, the eastern part continued until 1453. The Latin language survived, used by the Roman Catholic Church and by scientists and scholars across Europe. It is still learned today, and is the basis of languages such as Italian, Spanish, French and Romanian.

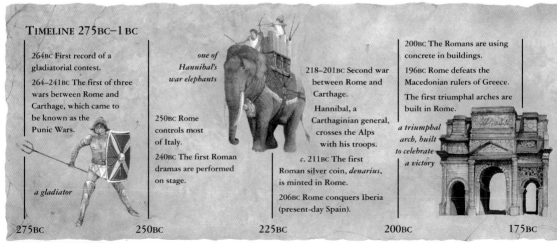

TIMELINE 275BC–1BC

264BC First record of a gladiatorial contest.

264–241BC The first of three wars between Rome and Carthage, which came to be known as the Punic Wars.

a gladiator

one of Hannibal's war elephants

250BC Rome controls most of Italy.

240BC The first Roman dramas are performed on stage.

218–201BC Second war between Rome and Carthage.

Hannibal, a Carthaginian general, crosses the Alps with his troops.

c. 211BC The first Roman silver coin, *denarius*, is minted in Rome.

206BC Rome conquers Iberia (present-day Spain).

200BC The Romans are using concrete in buildings.

196BC Rome defeats the Macedonian rulers of Greece.

The first triumphal arches are built in Rome.

a triumphal arch, built to celebrate a victory

275BC 250BC 225BC 200BC 175BC

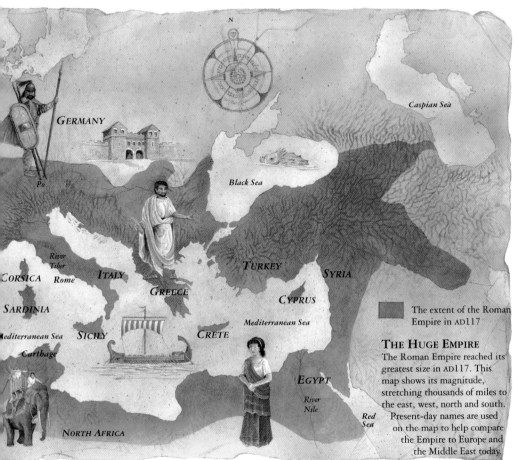

GERMANY

Caspian Sea

Po

Black Sea

River
Tiber
Rome

CORSICA   ITALY

SARDINIA

GREECE

TURKEY   SYRIA

CYPRUS

Mediterranean Sea

Mediterranean Sea   SICILY   CRETE

Carthage

EGYPT

River
Nile

Red
Sea

NORTH AFRICA

The extent of the Roman Empire in AD117

THE HUGE EMPIRE

The Roman Empire reached its greatest size in AD117. This map shows its magnitude, stretching thousands of miles to the east, west, north and south. Present-day names are used on the map to help compare the Empire to Europe and the Middle East today.

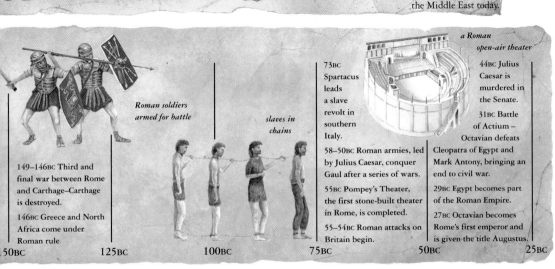

Roman soldiers armed for battle

slaves in chains

a Roman open-air theater

149–146BC Third and final war between Rome and Carthage–Carthage is destroyed.

146BC Greece and North Africa come under Roman rule.

73BC Spartacus leads a slave revolt in southern Italy.

58–50BC Roman armies, led by Julius Caesar, conquer Gaul after a series of wars.

55BC Pompey's Theater, the first stone-built theater in Rome, is completed.

55–54BC Roman attacks on Britain begin.

44BC Julius Caesar is murdered in the Senate.

31BC Battle of Actium – Octavian defeats Cleopatra of Egypt and Mark Antony, bringing an end to civil war.

29BC Egypt becomes part of the Roman Empire.

27BC Octavian becomes Rome's first emperor and is given the title Augustus.

150BC   125BC   100BC   75BC   50BC   25BC

The Roman World

THE PEOPLE who made Roman history came from many different backgrounds. The names of the famous survive on monuments and in books. There were consuls and emperors, successful generals and powerful politicians, great writers and historians. However, it was thousands of ordinary people who really kept the Roman Empire going—merchants, soldiers of the legions, tax collectors, servants, farmers, potters, and others like them.

Many of the most famous names of that time were not Romans at all. There was the Carthaginian general, Hannibal, Rome's deadliest enemy. There were also Celtic chieftains and queens, such as Vercingetorix, Caractacus and Boudicca.

ROMULUS AND REMUS
According to legend, Romulus was the founder and first king of Rome. The legend tells how he and his twin brother Remus were abandoned as babies. They were saved by a she-wolf, who looked after them until they were found by a shepherd.

AUGUSTUS (63BC–AD14)
Augustus, born Octavian, was the great-nephew and adopted son of Julius Caesar. After Caesar's death, he took control of the army. He became ruler of the Roman world after defeating Mark Antony at the Battle of Actium in 31BC. In 27BC, he became Rome's first emperor and was given the title Augustus.

CICERO (106–43BC)
Cicero is remembered as Rome's greatest orator, or speaker. Many of his letters and speeches still survive. He was a writer, poet, politician, lawyer and philosopher. He was elected consul of Rome in 63BC, but he had many enemies and was murdered in 43BC.

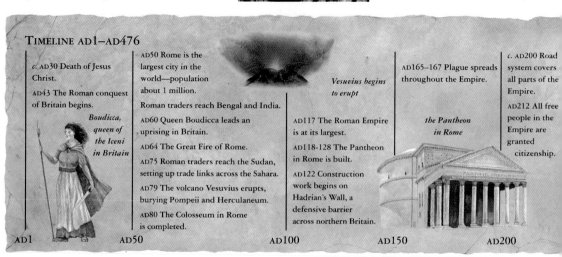

TIMELINE AD1–AD476

c. AD30 Death of Jesus Christ.

AD43 The Roman conquest of Britain begins.

Boudicca, queen of the Iceni in Britain

AD50 Rome is the largest city in the world—population about 1 million.

Roman traders reach Bengal and India.

AD60 Queen Boudicca leads an uprising in Britain.

AD64 The Great Fire of Rome.

AD75 Roman traders reach the Sudan, setting up trade links across the Sahara.

AD79 The volcano Vesuvius erupts, burying Pompeii and Herculaneum.

AD80 The Colosseum in Rome is completed.

Vesuvius begins to erupt

AD117 The Roman Empire is at its largest.

AD118-128 The Pantheon in Rome is built.

AD122 Construction work begins on Hadrian's Wall, a defensive barrier across northern Britain.

AD165–167 Plague spreads throughout the Empire.

the Pantheon in Rome

c. AD200 Road system covers all parts of the Empire.

AD212 All free people in the Empire are granted citizenship.

AD1   AD50   AD100   AD150   AD200

HADRIAN (AD76–138)

Hadrian became emperor in AD117 and spent many years traveling around the Empire. He had many splendid buildings constructed, as well as a defensive barrier across northern Britain, now known as Hadrian's Wall.

NERO (AD37–68) AND AGRIPPINA

Nero became emperor on the death of his adoptive father Claudius, in AD54. A cruel ruler, he was blamed for a great fire that destroyed much of Rome in AD64. Agrippina, his mother, was a powerful influence on him. She was suspected of poisoning two of her three husbands, and was eventually killed on her son's orders.

CLEOPATRA (68–30BC)

An Egyptian queen of Greek descent, Cleopatra had a son by Julius Caesar. She then fell in love with Mark Antony, a close follower of Caesar. They joined forces against Rome, but after a crushing defeat at Actium in 31BC, they both committed suicide. Egypt then became part of the Roman Empire.

JULIUS CAESAR (100–44BC)

Caesar was a talented and popular general and politician. He led Roman armies in an eight-year campaign to conquer Gaul (present-day France) in 50BC. In 49BC, he used his victorious troops to seize power and declare himself dictator for life. Five years later he was stabbed to death in the Senate by fellow politicians.

the cross, a symbol of Christianity

AD270 A new defensive wall is built around Rome by the Emperor Aurelian.

AD284 The Emperor Diocletian brings in new laws and taxes—divisions appear in the Empire.

AD313 Christianity is made legal in the Empire.

AD324 The Emperor Constantine reunites the Empire and founds the city of Constantinople (present-day Istanbul, in Turkey).

AD330 Constantine makes Constantinople his imperial residence and the new capital in the east.

AD395 The Roman Empire is divided again, this time into two parts—Eastern and Western.

AD410 The city of Rome is raided and ransacked by Visigoth armies from Germany.

the Emperor Constantine, depicted on a Roman coin

Vandal warrior

AD455 Vandal armies from Germany ransack Rome.

AD476 Fall of the Western Empire—the Eastern Empire survives until 1453.

D250   AD300   AD350   AD400   AD450

Rulers of Rome

I N THE EARLY DAYS, the city of Rome was ruled by kings. The first Roman king was said to be Romulus, the founder of the city in 753BC. The last king, a hated tyrant called Tarquinius the Proud, was thrown out in 509BC. The Romans then set up a republic. An assembly of powerful and wealthy citizens, the Senate, chose two consuls to lead them each year. By 493BC, the common people had their own representatives, too—the tribunes. In times of crisis, rulers could take on emergency powers and become dictators. The first Roman emperor, Augustus, was appointed by the Senate in 27BC. The emperors were given great powers and were even worshipped as gods. Some lived simply and ruled well, but others were violent, cruel men. They were surrounded by flatterers, and yet they lived in constant fear of plotters and murderers.

TRIUMPHAL PROCESSION
When a Roman general won a great victory, he was honored with a military parade called a triumph. Cheering crowds lined the streets as the grand procession passed by. If a general was successful and popular, the way to power was often open to him. Probably the most famous Roman ruler of all, Julius Caesar, came to power after a series of brilliant military conquests.

STATE SACRIFICE
Roman emperors had religious as well as political duties. As *pontifex maximus*, or high priest, an emperor would make sacrifices as offerings to the gods at important festivals.

figs

DEADLY FRUIT

Who killed Augustus, the first Roman emperor, in AD14? It is hard to say. It might have been a natural death... but then again, it might have been caused by his wife Livia. She was said to have coated the figs in his garden with a deadly poison. Roman emperors were much feared, but they were surrounded by enemies and could trust no one, least of all their own families.

PRAETORIAN GUARDS

The Praetorian Guards were the emperor's personal bodyguards. They wore special uniforms and were well paid. The guards were the only armed soldiers allowed within the city of Rome and so became very powerful. They also intervened in politics—assassinating the Emperor Caligula and electing his successor, Claudius.

In Rome, wreaths made from leaves of the laurel tree were worn by emperors, victorious soldiers and athletes. The wreath was a badge of honor. The Romans copied the idea from the ancient Greeks.

WREATH OF HONOR

You will need: tape measure, garden wire, pliers, scissors, clear tape, green ribbon, laurel leaves (real or fake).

1 Measure around your head with the tape measure. Cut some wire the same length, so the wreath will fit you. Bend the wire as shown and tape the ribbon around it.

2 Start to tape the leaves by their stems onto the wire, as shown above. Work your way around to the middle of the wire, fanning out the leaves as you go.

3 Then reverse the direction of the leaves and work your way around the rest of the wire. Fit the finished wreath around your head. Hail, Caesar!

Roman Society

ROMAN SOCIETY was never very fair. At first, a group of rich and powerful noble families, called the patricians, controlled the city and the Senate. Anyone who wanted their voice heard had to persuade a senator to speak on their behalf. Over the centuries the common citizens, known as plebeians, became more powerful until, by 287BC, they shared equally in government. Eventually, in the days of the Empire, even people of humble birth could become emperor, provided they were wealthy or had the support of the army. Emperors always feared riots by the common people of Rome, so they tried to keep the people happy with handouts of free food and lavish entertainments. Roman women had little power outside the family and could not vote. However, many were successful in business or had an important influence on political events. Slaves had very few rights, though Roman society depended on slave labor. Prisoners of war were bought and sold as slaves and many were treated cruelly, making slave revolts common.

A ROMAN CONSUL
This is a statue of a Roman consul, or leader of the Senate, in the days of the republic. At first, only the noble, and often wealthy, ruling class could be senators. However, under the emperors, the power and influence of the Senate slowly grew less and less.

LIFE AS A SLAVE
The everyday running of the Empire depended on slavery. This mosaic shows a young slave boy carrying fruit. In about AD100, a wealthy family might have had as many as 500 slaves. Some families treated their slaves well, and slaves who gave good service might earn their freedom. However, many more led miserable lives, toiling in the mines or laboring in the fields.

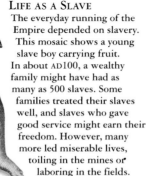

SLAVE TAG
This bronze disc was probably worn around the neck of a slave, like a dog-tag. The Latin words on it say: "Hold me, in case I run away, and return me to my master Viventius on the estate of Callistus." Slaves had few rights and could be branded on the forehead or leg as the property of their owners.

COLLECTING TAXES

This stone carving probably shows people paying their annual taxes. Officials counted the population of the Empire and registered them for paying tax. Money from taxes paid for the army and the government. However, many of the tax collectors took bribes, and even emperors seized public money to add to their private fortunes.

ARISTOCRATS

This Italian painting from the 1700s imagines how a noble Roman lady might dress after bathing. Wealthy people had personal slaves to help them bathe, dress and fix their hair. Household slaves were sometimes almost part of the family, and their children might be brought up and educated with their owner's children.

Country Life

THE FIRST ROMANS mostly lived by farming. Even when Rome had become a big city, Roman poets still liked to sing the praises of the countryside. In reality, country life was quite hard. Oxen were used for ploughing. Grain crops were harvested with a sickle, and flour was often ground by hand. Water had to be fetched by hand from the farm's well or a nearby spring.

Many farms were very small. They were often run by retired soldiers, who would raise chickens and geese and perhaps a cow or pig. They would also keep bees and grow olives and a few vegetables.

Other farms in Italy and across the Empire were large estates set up to provide incomes for their wealthy landowners. These estates might have their own olive presses, reaping machines and stores for drying grain. An estate was often laid out around a large, luxurious house or villa. Other villas were grand country houses owned by rich and powerful Romans.

A COUNTRY ESTATE
Life on a country estate was always busy, as this mosaic of a Roman villa in Tunisia, North Africa, shows. North African country estates supplied Rome with vast amounts of grain, fruit and vegetables. The good soil, combined with hot summers and rain in winter, made farming easy.

HADRIAN'S VILLA
One of the grandest country houses of all was built for the Emperor Hadrian between AD124 and 133. Parts of the villa still stand today, as this view of one of its lakeside walks shows. The luxurious villa itself stood on a hilltop, with Rome just visible in the distance. Built on land that belonged to Hadrian's family, the villa had pavilions and pools, terraces, banquet halls, theaters and libraries. All around the villa were parks filled with trees, such as laurels, planes and pines, exotic shrubs and formal flowerbeds. Hadrian designed the villa as a vacation palace where he could escape from the cares of government, but he died just four years after it was completed.

HUNTING WILD BOAR

Hunting scenes often decorated the walls of country villas. The hunt was a favorite pastime for young noblemen or army officers visiting the countryside. A wild boar, like the one shown in this mosaic, was one of the most dangerous animals of all when it charged.

FOOD FOR ROME

Rome needed huge amounts of food for all its people. Vegetables, such as leeks, celery, cabbage, beans and peas, were grown at market gardens around the city. Grain crops included wheat, barley, oats and rye. Grapes were made into wine and, as there was no sugar, honey was used to sweeten foods.

grapes

wheat

honey

GROVES OF OLIVE TREES

Olives were, and still are, an important crop in the lands around the Mediterranean. They were grown on small farms as well as on large estates. The oil was pressed and stored in large pottery jars. It was used for cooking or burned in oil lamps.

PLOUGHING THE LAND

This ploughman from Roman Britain is using a heavy wooden plough drawn by oxen. Large areas of Europe were still covered with thick forests in the days of the Roman Empire. Gradually farmers cleared land to plough, and farmland and orchards spread across the countryside.

Town and City

MANY OF THE TOWNS in Italy and the lands surrounding the Mediterranean Sea were already old and well established when the Romans invaded. Under Roman rule these towns prospered and grew. In other parts of Europe, where people had never lived in a big town, the Roman invaders built impressive new cities.

Roman towns had straight, paved roads planned on a grid pattern. Some were broad streets with pavements. Others were alleys just wide enough for a donkey. Most streets were busy with noisy crowds, street merchants, carts and rowdy bars. The streets divided the buildings into blocks called *insulae*, which means islands. The homes of wealthy families were spacious and comfortable. Poorer Romans often lived in apartment blocks that were badly built, crowded and in constant danger of burning down.

Fresh water was brought into towns through a system of channels called an aqueduct. The water was piped to fountains, public baths and to the homes of the wealthy.

THE STREETS OF POMPEII

On August 24, AD79, the volcano Vesuvius erupted violently, burying the Roman town of Pompeii in ash and lava. Work began in 1748 to excavate the ancient town, and its streets, shops and houses have slowly been revealed. In this excavated street, the deep ruts in the road made by cart wheels are clearly visible. Streets were often filled with mud and filth, so stepping-stones were laid for pedestrians to cross.

AN AQUEDUCT BRIDGE

You will need: ruler, pencil, scissors, thick and thin cardboard, white glue, paintbrush, masking tape, modeling clay, plaster of Paris, acrylic paints, water bowl.

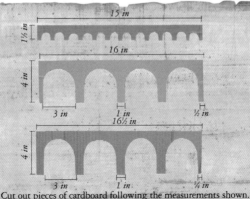

15 in
1½ in
16 in
4 in
3 in   1 in   ½ in
16½ in
4 in
3 in   1 in   ¼ in

Cut out pieces of cardboard following the measurements shown.

1 Draw and cut out the shapes of the arches from the thick cardboard. You need to cut out a pair for each level of the aqueduct— top, middle and bottom.

AQUEDUCTS

Water was carried into Roman towns and cities through a system of channels and pipes called aqueducts. Most of these were underground. Sometimes they were supported on high arches, such as this one, which still stands today in France. The water came from fresh springs, streams and lakes.

HERCULANEUM

The volcanic eruption that buried Pompeii caused a mud flow that buried a nearby coastal town, Herculaneum. Here, too, archaeologists have discovered houses, public baths, shops and workshops side by side on the city's streets. This view shows how crowded parts of the town were, with narrow paved streets separating the buildings.

CITY PLAN

This aerial view of Pompeii clearly shows how Roman streets were laid out on a grid pattern.

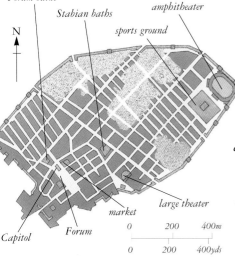

Forum baths

Stabian baths

amphitheater

sports ground

N

large theater

market

Capitol

Forum

| 0 | 200 | 400m |
| 0 | 200 | 400yds |

Aqueducts were built at a slight slope to ensure a steady flow of water. Arched bridges carried them across river valleys. The water flowed along a channel at the top of the bridge.

2 Cut strips of cardboard in three widths—1½ in, 1 in and ¾ in. These are for the insides of the arches. Use glue and tape to attach the 1½ in strips to the bottom.

3 Glue on the other side of the bottom level. Attach it with tape. Cut a top section from cardboard and glue and tape this on. Make the two other levels in the same way.

4 Roll the modeling clay into buttresses and wrap with cardboard. Attach these to the three central arches of the bottom level. These will support the aqueduct bridge.

5 Glue the levels together. Cover the model with plaster of Paris and mark on a brick pattern. Let dry. Paint the arches gray. Paint a blue channel of 'water' on top.

House and Garden

ONLY WEALTHY ROMANS could afford to live in a private house. A typical town house was designed to look inward, with the rooms arranged around a central courtyard and a walled garden. Outside walls had few windows and these were small and shuttered. The front door opened onto a short passage leading into an airy courtyard called an *atrium*. Front rooms on either side of the passage were usually used as bedrooms. Sometimes they were used as workshops or shops, having shutters that opened out onto the street.

The center of the atrium was open to the sky. Below this opening was a pool, set into the floor, to collect rainwater. Around the atrium were more bedrooms and the kitchen. If you were a guest or had important business you would be shown into the *tablinium*. The dining room, or *triclinium*, was often the grandest room of all. The very rich sometimes also had a summer dining room, which looked onto the garden.

Houses were made of locally available building materials. These might include stone, mud bricks, cement and timber. Roofs were made of clay tiles.

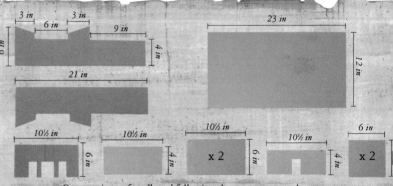

garden

bedroom

tablinium
(living room
and office)

LOCKS AND KEYS
This was the key to the door of a Roman house. Pushed in through a keyhole, the prongs at the end of the key fitted into holes in the bolt in the lock. The key could then be used to slide the bolt along and unlock the door.

INSIDE A ROMAN HOME
The outside of a wealthy Roman's town house was usually quite plain, but inside it was highly decorated with elaborate wall paintings and intricate mosaics. The rooms were sparsely furnished, with couches or beds, small side tables, benches and folding stools. There were few windows, but high ceilings and wide doors made the most of the light from the open atrium and the garden.

MAKE A ROMAN HOME
You will need: pencil, ruler, thick cardboard, scissors, white glue, paintbrushes, masking tape, corrugated cardboard, thin cardboard, water bowl, acrylic paints.

3 in   3 in
6 in
9 in
6 in
4 in
21 in
23 in
12 in
10½ in   6 in
10½ in
4 in
10½ in   x 2
6 in
10½ in
6 in
4 in   x 2

Cut out pieces of cardboard following the measurements shown.

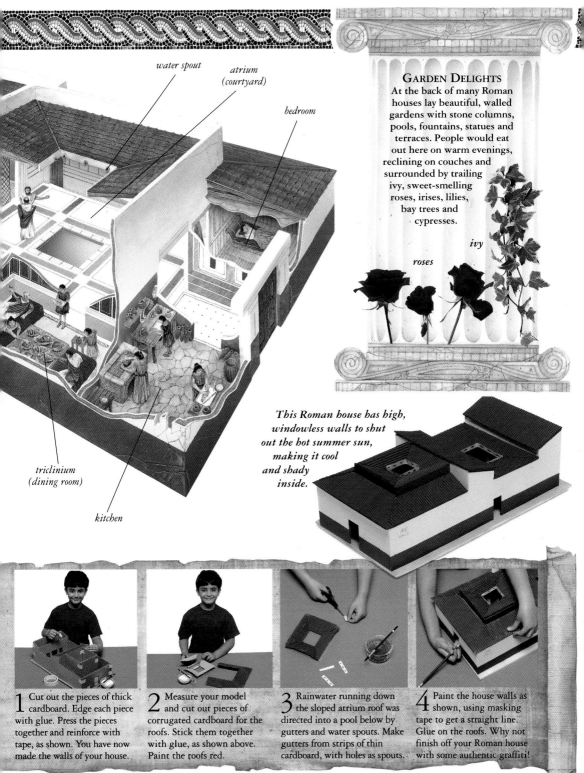

water spout

atrium
(courtyard)

bedroom

At the back of many Roman
houses lay beautiful, walled
gardens with stone columns,
pools, fountains, statues and
terraces. People would eat
out here on warm evenings,
reclining on couches and
surrounded by trailing
ivy, sweet-smelling
roses, irises, lilies,
bay trees and
cypresses.

ivy

roses

triclinium
(dining room)

kitchen

*This Roman house has high,
windowless walls to shut
out the hot summer sun,
making it cool
and shady
inside.*

1 Cut out the pieces of thick
cardboard. Edge each piece
with glue. Press the pieces
together and reinforce with
tape, as shown. You have now
made the walls of your house.

2 Measure your model
and cut out pieces of
corrugated cardboard for the
roofs. Stick them together
with glue, as shown above.
Paint the roofs red.

3 Rainwater running down
the sloped atrium roof was
directed into a pool below by
gutters and water spouts. Make
gutters from strips of thin
cardboard, with holes as spouts.

4 Paint the house walls as
shown, using masking
tape to get a straight line.
Glue on the roofs. Why not
finish off your Roman house
with some authentic graffiti!

Home Comforts

ROMAN HOUSES were less cluttered with furniture than our own. People kept their clothes in cupboards and wooden chests rather than in closets or drawers. Wooden or metal stools were used more than chairs. Couches were the most important piece of furniture, used for resting, eating and receiving visitors. Roman furniture was often simple, but rich people could afford fine, hand-crafted tables or benches made from wood, marble or bronze. Dining tables were very low, because wealthy Romans ate their evening meal lying on couches. Beds were often made of wood, with slats or ropes to support the mattress and pillows, which were stuffed with wool or straw.

Lighting in both rich and poor homes came from many small, flickering oil lamps made from clay or bronze. Heating came from charcoal burned in open braziers. The most luxurious houses were warmed by underfloor central heating, especially in colder parts of the Empire.

INTERIOR DECORATION
The walls, ceilings and floors of Roman houses were covered with paintings, mosaics and molded plaster reliefs. Elaborate scenes were painted directly onto the walls, while bright patterns in tiles and mosaics decorated the floor.

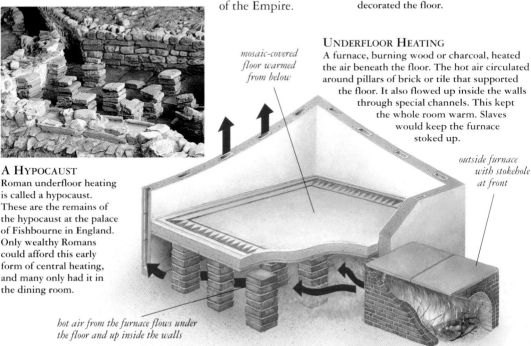

mosaic-covered floor warmed from below

UNDERFLOOR HEATING
A furnace, burning wood or charcoal, heated the air beneath the floor. The hot air circulated around pillars of brick or tile that supported the floor. It also flowed up inside the walls through special channels. This kept the whole room warm. Slaves would keep the furnace stoked up.

outside furnace with stokehole at front

A HYPOCAUST
Roman underfloor heating is called a hypocaust. These are the remains of the hypocaust at the palace of Fishbourne in England. Only wealthy Romans could afford this early form of central heating, and many only had it in the dining room.

hot air from the furnace flows under the floor and up inside the walls

HOUSEHOLD SHRINE

The *lararium*, or household shrine, was a small private altar containing images of the family's ancestors. It was usually situated in the *atrium* at the center of the house. Every day the family would honor their ancestors by burning incense at the shrine.

DINNER IS SERVED

These are guests at a banquet in Roman Germany. Only country folk, foreigners and slaves ate sitting upright at the table. Tables and chairs were usually made of wood and might be carved or painted. There were also woven wicker armchairs. Wealthy Romans ate lying on couches around a central low table.

LAMPLIGHT

Roman homes glowed with the soft light of candles and oil lamps. Lamps were made of pottery or bronze, like this one. They came in many different designs, but they all had a central well containing olive oil. The oil was soaked up by a wick, which provided a steady flame. Sometimes lamps would be grouped together or hung from a tall lampstand.

A LUXURY TO LIE ON

This beautifully decorated bed is made from wood inlaid with ivory and semi-precious stones. It dates back to about 50BC, and was discovered in the remains of a villa in Italy. The villa had been buried under ash from a volcanic eruption. Beds, or couches for sleeping on, were much higher than ours are today and people needed steps or a stool to get up on them.

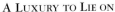

In the Kitchen

WHEN A LARGE MEAL was being prepared, slaves would have to carry water and fresh kindling for the fire into the kitchen. As the fires were lit, the room would become quite smoky because there was no chimney. Soon the coals would be glowing red hot and pots would be boiling on trivets and griddles on the raised brick stove. Food was boiled, fried, grilled and stewed. Larger kitchens might include stone ovens for baking bread or spits for roasting meat. A few even had piped hot water.

The kitchens of wealthy Romans were well equipped with all kinds of bronze pots, pans, strainers and ladles. Pottery storage jars held wine, olive oil and sauces. Herbs, vegetables and cuts of meat hung from hooks in the roof. There were no airtight containers, and no fridges or freezers to keep food fresh. Food had to be preserved in oil or by drying, smoking, salting or pickling.

mortar

VALUABLE GLASS
This glass bottle or pitcher was made about 1,900 years ago. Precious liquids or expensive perfumes were sold in bottles like this throughout the Empire. When a bottle was empty, it was far too valuable to throw away, so it was often reused to store food such as honey in the kitchen.

MORTAR AND PESTLE
The Romans liked spicy food. Roman cooks used a mortar and pestle to grind up foods, such as nuts, herbs and spices, into a paste. Both pieces were usually made of a very tough pottery or stone. The rough inside of the mortar was made of coarse grit to help grind the food.

pestle

A ROMAN KITCHEN

You will need: pencil, ruler, cardboard, scissors, paintbrush, white glue, masking tape, water bowl, acrylic paints, red felt tip pen, plaster of Paris, balsa wood, sandpaper, self-drying clay, work board, modeling tool.

1 Cut out the walls and floor of the kitchen from cardboard, as shown. Glue the edges and press them together. Reinforce the walls with pieces of masking tape.

2 Paint the floor gray. When dry, use the ruler and pencil to draw on stone flags. Paint the walls yellow, edged with blue. When dry, use the felt tip pen to draw stripes.

3 Cut out pieces of cardboard to make a stove about ¾ in long, 2 in wide and 1½ in high. Glue the pieces together and reinforce with masking tape, as shown above.

READY FOR THE COOK

Herbs brought fresh from the garden included cilantro, oregano, rue, mint, thyme and parsley. Food was spiced with pepper, caraway, aniseed, mustard seeds and saffron. On the table there might be eggs, grapes, figs and nuts. Much of our knowledge of Roman cooking comes from recipes collected by a Roman gourmet called Apicius nearly 2,000 years ago.

saffron

thyme

mint

quails' eggs

BAKING PAN

This bronze tray was probably used as a mold for baking honey cakes, buns or pastries. The long handle makes it easier to remove from a hot oven. It may also have been used to cook eggs.

STRAINER

This bronze strainer was used by Roman cooks to strain sauces. It was made using the same design as a saucepan, but its bowl has been pierced with an intricate pattern. The hole in the handle was used to hang it from a hook on the wall.

SAUCEPAN

Like many Roman kitchen utensils, this saucepan is made from bronze. Bronze contains copper, which can give food a very strange flavor—the inside of the saucepan has been coated with silver to prevent this from happening.

Foods in a Roman kitchen were stored in baskets, bowls or sacks. Wine, oil and sauces were stored in pottery jars called amphorae.

4 Coat the stove with plaster of Paris. Let dry. Then, use sandpaper to rub it smooth. Make a grate from two strips of cardboard and four pieces of balsa wood, glued together.

5 Use the acrylic paints to color the stove and the grate, as shown above. Use small pieces of balsa wood to make a pile of wood fuel to store underneath the stove.

6 Make a table and shelves from balsa wood, as shown. Glue them together, and bind with masking tape. Let them dry before painting the pieces brown.

7 Use the clay to form pots, pans, bowls, storage jars, perhaps even a frying pan or an egg poacher. Let the utensils dry before painting them a suitable color.

Food and Drink

FOR POOR ROMANS, a meal was often little more than a hurried bowl of porridge or a crust of bread washed down with sour wine. Many town-dwellers lived in homes without kitchens. They ate take-out meals bought at the many food stalls and bars in town. Even for wealthier people, breakfast might be just a quick snack of bread, honey and olives. Lunch, too, was a light meal, perhaps of eggs or cold meats and fruit. The main meal of the day was *cena*, or dinner. This evening meal might start with shellfish or a salad, followed by a main course of roast meat, such as pork, veal, chicken or goose, with vegetables. It finished with a dessert course of fruit or honey cakes.

More lavish banquets might include fattened dormice, songbirds, flamingos' tongues or a custard made from calves' brains and rose hips! Food was heavily spiced and was often served with a fish sauce called *garum*. Wine was usually mixed with water and sometimes flavored with honey or spices. Guests could take home any tasty morsels that were left over.

SERVING SLAVES
This mosaic shows a slave called Paregorius helping to prepare his master's table for a banquet. On his head he is carrying a tray with plates of food. During a banquet, dishes were brought in a few at a time and set down on a small table. All the food was cooked and served by slaves.

HONEYED DATES

You will need: cutting board, dates, small knife, walnuts, pecans, almonds, hazelnuts, mortar and pestle, salt, 1 cup of honey, frying pan, wooden spoon, a few fresh mint leaves.

1 On the cutting board, slit open the dates with the knife. Remove the pit inside. Be sure not to cut the dates completely in half and be careful with the knife.

2 Put aside the hazelnuts. Chop up the rest of the nuts. Use a mortar and pestle to grind them into smaller pieces. Stuff a small amount into the middle of each date.

3 Pour some of the salt onto the cutting board and lightly roll each date in it. Make sure the dates are coated all over, but do not use too much salt.

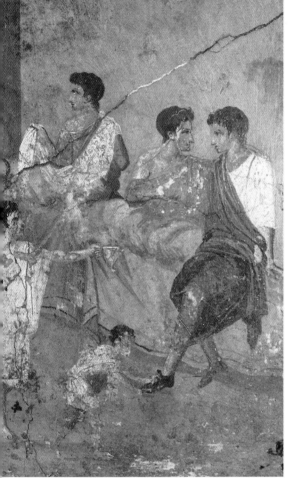

CUPS

Pottery cups like this one were used for drinking wine. Many drinking cups had handles and were often highly decorated. Metal cups could make wine taste unpleasant, so colored glass cups and pottery cups were more popular.

THE FAMILY SILVER

These silver spoons were used by a wealthy family in Roman Britain. Food was usually eaten with the fingers, but spoons were used for sauces. At banquets, Romans liked to bring out their best silver tableware as a sign of status.

AT A BANQUET

This wall painting shows a typical Roman banquet. Guests usually sat three to a couch. After the meal they were entertained with poetry readings and music, or jokes and jugglers. Dress and table manners were very important at a banquet. Arguments and bad language were not allowed, but it was fine to spit, belch or even eat until you were sick!

4 Over a low heat, melt the honey in the frying pan. Lightly fry the dates for five minutes, turning them with a wooden spoon. Be careful while using the stove.

5 Arrange the stuffed dates in a shallow dish. Sprinkle on the whole hazelnuts, some chopped nuts and a few leaves of fresh mint. Now they are ready to serve to your friends.

The Romans loved sweet dishes made from nuts and dates imported from North Africa. They also used dates to make sauces for savory dishes such as fish and roast duck.

Getting Dressed

MOST ROMAN CLOTHES were made of wool that had been spun and woven by hand at home or in a workshop. Flax was grown in Egypt to make linen, while cotton from India and silk from China were rare and expensive imports. The most common style of clothing was a simple tunic, which was practical for people who led active lives, such as workers, slaves and children. Important men also wore a white robe called a toga. This was a 6-yard length of cloth with a curved edge, wrapped around the body and draped over the shoulder. It was heavy and uncomfortable to wear, but looked very impressive. Women wore a long dress called a *stola*, over an under-tunic. Often they also wore a *palla*—a large shawl that could be arranged in various ways. Girls wore white until they were married, after which they often wore dresses dyed in bright colors.

DRESSING FOR DIONYSUS

Wall paintings in the homes of wealthy Romans hold many clues about the way people dressed in the Roman world. This scene was found in the Villa of the Mysteries, in Pompeii. It shows young women being prepared as ceremonial brides for Dionysus, the god of wine.

ROMAN FOOTWEAR

This sandal (*left*) and child's shoe (*far left*) were found in York, in Britain. Most Romans wore open leather sandals. There were many different designs, and some had nailed soles to make them harder wearing. Shoes and boots were worn in the colder parts of the Empire.

WEAR A TOGA

You will need: old white sheet, tape measure, scissors for cutting cloth and tape, double-sided tape, purple ribbon, long T-shirt, cord.

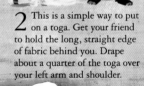

1 Ask a friend to help you with the toga. Wealthy Romans had slaves to help them put on their togas. Fold the sheet in half along its length. Cut the ends to make rounded corners at each end, as shown. Use double-sided tape to stick the ribbon along the long edge. Put on a long, white T-shirt tied at the waist with cord.

2 This is a simple way to put on a toga. Get your friend to hold the long, straight edge of fabric behind you. Drape about a quarter of the toga over your left arm and shoulder.

WORKERS' CLOTHES

Not all Romans wore flowing robes. This man is probably a farm worker from Roman Germany. He wears strips of cloth around his legs and a hooded leather cloak to protect him from the cold, wet weather. Hooded cloaks like this were exported from Gaul (present-day France) and Britain.

DRESSED TO IMPRESS

This stone carving shows the family of the Emperor Augustus, dressed for an important state occasion. The women are all shown wearing a *stola*, with a *palla* draped around their shoulders or head. The men and boys are shown in togas. A toga could be worn by all free Roman citizens, but only the wealthy upper classes wore it. This was because it took time—and a helping hand—to put on a toga. Once you had it on, it was also quite awkward to move in!

Boys from wealthy families wore togas edged with a thin purple stripe until they reached the age of 16. They then wore plain togas. A toga with a broad purple stripe was worn by Roman senators. Purple dye was expensive, so the color was only worn by high-ranking citizens.

3 Bring the rest of the toga around to the front, passing it under your right arm. Hook the toga up by tucking a few folds of material securely into the cord around your waist.

4 Now your friend can help you fold the rest of the toga neatly over your left arm, as shown above. If you prefer, you could drape it all over your left shoulder.

Fashion and Beauty

A ROMAN LADY would spend most of the morning surrounded by her female slaves. Some would bring her a mirror made of bronze or silver and jars of perfumed oils or ointments. Another slave would comb out her hair—and could expect a spiteful jab with a hairpin if she pulled at a tangle.

Most rich women wanted to look pale—after all, only women who had to work outdoors became sunburned. So chalk, or even a poisonous powder made from white lead, was rubbed into the face. Face packs were made of bread and milk. One remedy for spots and pimples included bird droppings! Lipsticks and blusher were made of red ocher or the sediment from red wine. Eyeshadow was made of ash and saffron. Women's hair was curled, braided or pinned up, according to the latest fashion.

PORTRAIT OF A LADY
This is a portrait of a lady who lived in the Roman province of Egypt. Her earrings and necklace are made of emeralds, garnets and pearls set in gold. They are a sign of her wealth, as they would have been very expensive. Her hair has been curled, and lampblack or soot may have been used to darken her eyelashes and eyebrows.

CARVED COMB
This comb is carved from ivory and is inscribed in Latin with the words "Modestina farewell." Combs of silver and ivory were used to decorate the intricate hairstyles favored by many Roman women. The poor used wooden or bone combs, though more out of need than fashion.

SCENT BOTTLES
These lovely perfume bottles belonged to a Roman lady. The round one is made of hand-blown, gold-banded glass. The other is carved from onyx, a precious stone with layers of different colors.

A GOLDEN HEADDRESS
You will need: tape measure, plain cardboard, pencil, scissors, white glue, paintbrush, string, plastic beads, gold foil wrappers, tape or paper clip.

1 Measure around your head with the tape measure. Draw the shape of the tiara to the same length on cardboard. Also draw outlines for various sizes of leaf shape, as shown.

2 Carefully cut out the tiara outline from the cardboard. Also cut out the leaf shapes. Then cut out the center of each one so that they look a bit like arches.

3 Use the white glue and a paintbrush to paste the shapes securely onto the front of the tiara. These will be part of an elegant pattern for your tiara.

CROWNING GLORY

This lady's elaborately curled hair is almost certainly a wig. Hairpieces and wigs were always popular with wealthy Roman women—a bride would wear at least six layers of artificial hair at her wedding. Wigs of black hair were usually imported from Asia, while blond or red hair came from northern Europe.

MEN'S CHANGING HAIRSTYLES

Roman men were just as concerned with their appearance as women. They usually wore their hair short, either combed forward or curled. They were mostly clean shaven, but beards became fashionable during the reign of the Emperor Hadrian, AD117–138.

A FINE DISPLAY

This picture shows a ceremonial dance at the Temple of the Sun in Rome. Both the men and women are wearing golden headdresses decorated with precious jewels and gold filigree. Lavish displays like this were reserved for grand public occasions to show off the wealth and power of the Empire.

RINGS ON THEIR FINGERS

Both men and women wore jewelry, especially rings. Rich people would wear rings like these, usually made of gold or silver. Emeralds, pearls and amber were also used in rings. The less wealthy would wear rings of bronze.

4 Cut lengths of string and glue them around the inside edges of the shapes. Glue plastic beads at the top of each arch, so that they look like precious stones.

5 Collect gold foil candy wrappers and glue them onto the tiara. Use the end of the paintbrush to carefully poke the foil into all the corners around the beads.

The finished tiara can be held together at the back by tape or a paper clip. Roman ladies liked to wear tiaras made of gold, with jewels in their hair.

Lessons and Learning

MOST CHILDREN in the Roman Empire never went to school. They learned a trade from their parents or found out about sums by trading on a market stall. Boys might be trained to fight with swords or to ride horses, in preparation for joining the army. Girls would be taught how to run the home, in preparation for marriage.

Wealthy families did provide an education for their sons and sometimes for their daughters, too. They were usually taught at home by a private tutor, but there were also small schools. Tutors and schoolmasters would teach children arithmetic, and how to read and write in both Latin and Greek. Clever pupils might also learn public speaking skills, poetry and history. Girls often had music lessons at home, on a harp-like instrument called a lyre.

INKPOTS AND PENS
Pen and ink were used to write on scrolls made from papyrus (a kind of reed) or thin sheets of wood. Ink was often made from soot or lampblack, mixed with water. It was kept in inkpots such as these. Inkpots were made from glass, pottery or metal. Pens were made from bone, reeds or bronze.

WRITING IN WAX
This painting shows a couple from Pompeii. The man holds a parchment scroll. His wife is probably going through their household accounts. She holds a wax-covered writing tablet and a stylus to scratch words into the wax. A stylus had a pointed end for writing and a flat end for erasing.

A WRITING TABLET
You will need: sheets and sticks of balsa wood, craft knife, ruler, white glue, paintbrush, brown acrylic paint, water bowl, modeling clay, work board, rolling pin, modeling tool, skewer, purple thread, pencil (to be used as a stylus), gold paint.

1 Use the craft knife to cut the balsa sheet into two rectangles 4 in x 9 in. The sticks of balsa should be cut into four lengths 9 in long and four lengths 4 in long.

2 Glue the sticks around the edges of each sheet as shown. These form a shallow hollow into which you can press the "wax." Paint the two frames a rich brown color.

3 Roll out the modeling clay on a board and place a balsa frame on top. Use the modeling tool to cut around the outside of the frame. Repeat this step.

TEACHER AND PUPILS

This stone sculpture from Roman Germany shows a teacher seated between two of his pupils. They are reading their lessons from papyrus scrolls. Children had to learn poetry and other writings by heart. Any bad behavior or mistakes were punished with a beating.

WRITING IT DOWN

Various materials were used for writing. Melted beeswax was poured into wooden trays to make writing tablets. Letters were scratched into the wax, which could be used again and again. Powdered soot was mixed with water and other ingredients to make ink for writing on papyrus, parchment or wood.

soot

melted beeswax

Roman numerals on papyrus

LETTERS IN STONE

Temples, monuments and public buildings were covered in Latin inscriptions, such as this one. Each letter was beautifully chiseled by a stonemason. These words are carved in marble and were made to mark the 14th birthday of Lucius Caesar, the grandson of the Emperor Augustus.

4 Cut off about ½ in all around the edge of each modeling clay rectangle. This helps to make sure that the modeling clay will fit inside the balsa wood frame.

5 Carefully press the clay into each side—this represents the wax. Use the skewer to poke two holes through the inside edge of each frame; as shown.

6 Join the two frames together by threading purple thread through each pair of holes and tying it securely together. You have now made your tablet.

Paint the pencil gold to make it look as if it is made of metal. Use it like a stylus to scratch words on your tablet. Why not try writing in Latin? You could write CIVIS ROMANVS SVM, which means "I am a Roman citizen."

31

In the Forum

EVERY LARGE ROMAN TOWN had a forum—a market square with public buildings around it. This was where people gathered to do business and exchange friendly gossip. In the morning, while the lady of the house had her hair done and her children struggled with their lessons, her husband would walk over to the forum.

In the forum's central square, crowds thronged around market stalls. Sometimes a public fight might break out, as inspectors of weights and measures accused some trader of cheating his customers. Around the square were shops, imposing monuments, marble statues and temples to the gods. The walls of buildings were often scrawled with graffiti made up of political messages, personal insults or declarations of love. On one side of the forum was the basilica, a large building used as the town hall, a court of law and public meeting place. Some of the crowds may have been members of the *curia* or town council, or one of the trade guilds who had their halls there.

DOWNTOWN POMPEII
The ruins at Pompeii include these remains of a row of columns. They were part of a two-story colonnade that once took up three sides of the forum. Rows of shops and market stalls were set up behind the colonnade at ground level.

TEMPLES AND PROSPERITY
The forum of every town had splendid temples to the many gods and goddesses of ancient Rome. There were also temples for famous Romans. The grand columns of this temple still remain in the forum at Rome. Today, a Christian church stands behind it. The temple was built in honor of Antoninus Pius, one of Rome's wisest emperors, and his wife Faustina.

MAKING MONEY

Money changers and bankers gathered to make deals and discuss business in the forum. Here, too, tax collectors raised money for the town council—taxes were charged on all goods that passed through the town.

FAST FOOD

As people hurried to work or chatted with friends, they might pick up a snack at a food stall or a street vendor. Pastries filled with spicy meats made popular snacks. On market day, the forum would also be busy with traders and farmers setting up stalls in the central square.

THE BASILICA

This is the Basilica of Maxentius in Rome. A basilica was a huge building used as a cross between a town hall and a court of law. It usually had a very high roof, supported by rows of columns. The columns divided the building into a central area with two side aisles. People came here to work, do business or simply chat with friends.

Shopping—Roman Style

I**N MOST LARGE TOWNS**, shops spread out from the forum and along the main streets. Shops were usually small, family-run businesses. At the start of the working day, shutters or blinds would be taken from the shop front and goods put on display. Noise would soon fill the air as bakers, butchers, fishmongers, fruit and vegetable sellers all began crying out that their produce was the best and cheapest. Cuts of meat might be hung from a pole, while ready-cooked food, grains or oils would be sold from pots set into a stone counter. Other shops sold pottery lamps or bronze lanterns, kitchen pots and pans or knives, while some traders repaired shoes or laundered cloth. Hammering and banging coming from the workshops at the back added to the clamor of a busy main street.

HOW'S BUSINESS?
This carving shows merchants discussing prices and profits while an assistant brings out goods from the stockroom. Most Roman shops were single rooms, with stores or workshops at the back.

ROMAN MONEY
The same currency was used throughout the Roman Empire. Coins were made of gold, silver and bronze. Shoppers kept their money in purses made of cloth or leather or in wooden boxes.

GOING TO MARKET
This is a view of Trajan's Market, a multistory group of shops set into a hillside in Rome. Most Roman towns had covered halls or central markets like this, where shops were rented out to traders.

A ROMAN DELICATESSEN

About 1,700 years ago this was the place to buy good food in Ostia, the seaport nearest Rome. Bars, inns and cafés had stone counters that were often decorated with colored marble. At lunchtime, bars like this would be busy with customers enjoying a meal.

A BUTCHER'S SHOP

A Roman butcher uses a cleaver to prepare chops while a customer waits for her order. Butchers' shops have changed very little over the ages—pork, lamb and beef were sold, and sausages were popular, too. On the right hangs a steelyard, a metal bar with a pan like a scale, for weighing the meat.

DISHING IT UP

These are the remains of a shop that sold food. Set into the marble counter are big pottery containers, called *dolia*. These were used for displaying and serving up food, such as beans and lentils. They were also used for keeping jars of wine cool on hot summer days. The containers could be covered with wooden or stone lids to keep out the flies.

Trades and Crafts

THERE WERE POTTERY WORKSHOPS throughout the Roman Empire. Clay pots were made by turning and shaping wet clay on a wheel and baking it in a kiln. Some of the best clay came from the district of Arretium, in Italy. Large pottery centers in Gaul (present-day France) produced a very popular red pottery called Samian ware. In Roman Germany, pottery drinking cups were colored black and decorated in white with mottoes such as "Drink Up!" or "Bring Me Wine!"—in Latin, of course!

The Romans learned from the Syrians how to blow glass into shapes on the end of a long tube. This was a new and simple technique, although ways of making glass had been known for centuries. As a result, glass became widely used in Roman times.

The skills of the blacksmith were called for everyday, all over the Empire. Smiths hammered away on their anvils, shaping iron tools, weapons and pots. Some metalworkers were fine artists, working in gold, silver and bronze.

THE BLACKSMITHS' GOD
The Romans believed in many different gods. This is a statue of Vulcan, the god of smiths, or metal-workers. He is holding a hammer, used to shape hot metal on an anvil.

COPPERSMITHS
A typical busy day at a coppersmiths' workshop. A customer and his son look on as one of the smiths hammers out sheets of hot copper on an anvil. Another smith is bent over his work, decorating a copper bowl. The goods they are selling are displayed on the wall and hung from the ceiling.

SAMIAN POTTERY

This decorated bowl was found at Felixstowe, in Britain. Glossy red Samian ware was made in Gaul (present-day France), in workshops almost as big as factories. This popular pottery was transported all over the Empire, by land and by sea.

ROMAN SHOP

This stone carving shows a Roman shop with cloth and cushions for sale. Customers are seated while the shopkeeper shows them his wares. The Romans were skilled sculptors, and much of our knowledge about the Empire comes from detailed carvings in stone such as this one.

ROMAN GLASSMAKING

Quality glass was made into bowls, pitchers, flasks and bottles. Some were very simple in design, while others were highly decorated. Bands of colored glass and even gold were used in some pieces. The finest glassware was used by wealthy Romans, and was always brought out when they entertained guests.

NATURAL DYES

Roman textile workers used a variety of natural dyes on cloth, including onion skins (a golden-yellow dye), pine cones (a reddish-yellow dye) and tree bark (a reddish-brown dye). Other natural sources included berries, leaves, minerals, shellfish, nettles and saffron from crocuses.

bark

onion

pine cones

Pictures and Statues

THE ROMANS loved to decorate their homes and public places with paintings and statues. Mosaics were pictures made using *tesserae*—cubes of stone, pottery or glass—which were pressed into soft cement. Mosaic pictures might show hunting scenes, the harvest or Roman gods. Geometric patterns were popular and often used as borders.

Wall paintings, or murals, often showed garden scenes, birds and animals or heroes and goddesses. They were painted onto wooden panels or directly onto the wall. Roman artists loved to trick the eye by painting false columns, archways and shelves.

The Romans were skilled sculptors, using stone, marble and bronze. They imitated the ancient Greeks in putting up marble statues in public places and gardens. These might be of gods and goddesses or emperors and generals.

A COUNTRY SCENE
This man and wild boar are part of a mosaic made in Roman North Africa. Making a mosaic was quite tricky—a lot like doing a jigsaw puzzle. Even so, skilled artists could create lifelike scenes from chips of colored glass, pottery and stone.

SCULPTURE
Statues of metal or stone were often placed in gardens. This bronze figure is in the remains of a house in Pompeii. It is of a faun, a god of the countryside.

FLOOR MOSAICS
Birds, animals, plants and country scenes were popular subjects for mosaics. These parrots are part of a much larger, and quite elaborate, floor mosaic from a Roman house.

MAKE A MOSAIC

You will need: rough paper, pencil, ruler, scissors, large sheet of cardboard, self-drying clay, rolling pin, work board, modeling knife, acrylic paints, paintbrush, water bowl, varnish and brush (optional), plaster of Paris, spreader, muslin rag.

1 Sketch out your mosaic design on rough paper. A design like this one is good to start with. Cut the cardboard so it measures 10 in x 4 in. Copy the design onto it.

2 Roll out the clay on the board. Use the ruler to measure out small squares on the clay. Cut them out with the modeling knife. Let dry. These will be your tesserae.

3 Paint the pieces in batches of different colors, as shown above. When the paint is dry, you can coat them with clear varnish for extra strength and shine. Let dry.

MOSAIC MATERIALS

Mosaics were often made inside frames, in workshops, and then transported to where they were to be used. Sometimes, the tesserae were brought to the site and fitted on the spot by the workers. The floor of an average room in a Roman town house might need over 100,000 pieces.

tesserae

pot shards

MUSICIANS AND DANCERS

This dramatic painting is on the wall of an excavated villa in Pompeii. It is one in a series of paintings that show the secret rites, or mysteries, honoring the god Dionysus.

REAL OR FAKE?

Roman artists liked to make painted objects appear real enough to touch. This bowl of fruit on a shelf is typical of this style of painting. It was found on the wall of a villa that belonged to a wealthy Roman landowner.

4 Spread the plaster of Paris onto the cardboard, a small part at a time. While it is still wet, press in your tesserae following the design, as shown. Use your sketch as a guide.

5 When the mosaic is dry, use the muslin rag to polish up the surface. Any other soft, dry cloth would also be suitable. Now your mosaic is ready for display.

The Romans liked to have mosaics in their homes. Wealthy people often had elaborate mosaics in their courtyards and dining rooms, as these were rooms that visitors would see.

Doctors and Medicine

SOME ROMANS lived to a ripe old age, but most died
before they reached the age of 50. Archaeologists have
found out a lot about health and disease in Roman times by
examining skeletons that have survived. They can tell, for
example, how old a person was when they died and their
general state of health during their life. Ancient writings
also provide information about Roman medical knowledge.

Roman doctors knew very little science. They
healed the sick through a mixture of common sense,
trust in the gods and magic. Most cures and
treatments had come to Rome from the doctors
of ancient Greece. The Greeks and Romans
also shared the same god of healing,
Aesculapius. There were doctors in most
parts of the Empire, as well as midwives, dentists
and eye specialists. Surgeons operated on wounds
received in battle, on broken bones and even skulls.

The only pain killers were made from
poppy juice—an operation must have
been a terrible ordeal.

A CHEMIST'S SHOP
This pharmacy, or chemist's shop, is
run by a woman. This was quite
unusual for Roman times, as
women were rarely given positions
of responsibility. Roman
pharmacists collected herbs
and often mixed them
for doctors.

**GODDESS
OF HEALTH**
Greeks and Romans
honored the daughter of the god
Aesculapius as a goddess of
health. She was called Hygieia.
The word hygienic, which comes
from her name, is still used today
to mean free of germs.

MEDICINE BOX
Boxes like this one
would have been used
by Roman doctors to
store various drugs.
Many of the
treatments used by
doctors were herbal,
and not always
pleasant to take.

MEDICAL INSTRUMENTS
The Romans used a variety of surgical
and other instruments. These are made
in bronze and include a scalpel, forceps
and a spatula for mixing and applying
various ointments.

TAKING THE CURE

These are the ruins of a medical clinic in Asia Minor (present-day Turkey). It was built around AD150, in honor of Aesculapius, the god of healing. Clinics like this one were known as therapy buildings. People would come to them seeking cures for all kinds of ailments.

BATHING THE BABY

This stone carving from Rome shows a newborn baby being bathed. The Romans were well aware of the importance of regular bathing in clean water. However, childbirth itself was dangerous for both mother and baby. Despite the dangers, the Romans liked to have large families, and many women died giving birth.

HERBAL MEDICINE

Doctors and traveling healers sold all kinds of potions and ointments. Many were made from herbs such as rosemary, sage and fennel. Other natural remedies included garlic, mustard and cabbage. Many of the remedies would have done little good, but some of them did have the power to heal.

garlic

sage

rosemary

Keeping Clean

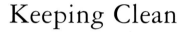

tepidarium (warm room)

THE ROMANS may not have all enjoyed good health, but they did like to keep clean. There were public toilets, flushed with constantly flowing water, and people regularly visited public baths. Most towns, even military bases on the frontiers of the Empire, had public bath houses.

The baths were more than just places to wash in. Bathers would meet their friends and spend the afternoon gossiping, in between dips in the bathing pools. Others would exercise, play ball games or just relax. Businessmen even held meetings at the baths. Men and women used separate rooms or visited the bath house at different times. Slaves would bring bath towels and wooden-soled sandals. Bathers needed the sandals because many of the rooms had hot floors heated by a system of underfloor heating.

OIL FLASK AND STRIGILS
Romans used olive oil instead of soap. They would rub themselves with oil and scrape it off with a curved metal tool called a strigil. The oil would be kept in a small flask, like this one, which has two strigils chained to it.

warm air ducts in walls

BATHING AT BATH
This is a view of the Roman baths in the town of Bath, in Britain. The Romans built the baths there because of the natural hot spring, which bubbled up from the rocks at temperatures of up to 122°F. Rich in health-giving minerals, it attracted visitors from far and wide. This large lead-lined pool was used for swimming. In Roman times, it was covered by a roof.

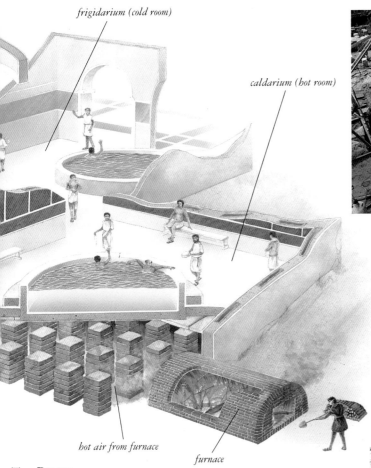

frigidarium (cold room)

caldarium (hot room)

hot air from furnace

furnace

BATH HOUSE DIG
An archaeological dig in Britain has uncovered these remains of the foundations of a bath house. You can see the bottoms of the pillars that once supported the floor. Hot air from a furnace would have flowed around these pillars, heating the floor and the rooms above it.

THE BATHS
The public baths included exercise areas, changing rooms, a sauna and various pools. The rooms and water were heated by hot air from one or more underground furnaces. The *frigidarium*, or cold room, usually had an unheated pool for bathers to take an icy plunge and was often partly open-air. It led onto a warmer area, the *tepidarium*. In the warmth, bathers would rub themselves with oil, then scrape off any dirt or grime. When they were clean, they were ready to take a dip in the pool. The steamy *caldarium*, or hot room, was nearest to a furnace. Here, bathers could soak or sweat to their hearts' content.

PUBLIC TOILETS
The remains of public toilets like these have been found in many parts of the Empire. People used sponges on sticks to clean themselves. They could rinse the sponges in a channel of flowing water in front of them. Another channel of water, under the stone seats, carried away the waste.

Sport and Combat

MOST ROMANS preferred watching sport rather than taking part themselves. There were some, however, who enjoyed athletics and keeping fit. They took their exercise at the public baths and at the sports ground or *palaestra*. Men would compete at wrestling, long jump and swimming. Women would work out with weights.

Boxing matches and chariot races were always well attended. The races took place on a long, oval racetrack, called a circus. The crowds would watch with such excitement that violent riots often followed. Charioteers and their teams became big stars. Roman crowds also enjoyed watching displays of cruelty. Bloody battles between gladiators and fights among wild animals took place in a special oval arena, called an amphitheater. Roman entertainments became more spectacular and bloodthirsty as time passed. They would even flood the arenas of amphitheaters for mock sea battles.

A COLOSSEUM
This is the colosseum in the Roman city of El Djem, in Tunisia. A colosseum was a kind of amphitheater. Arenas such as this were built all over the Empire. The largest and most famous is the Colosseum in Rome.

DEATH OR MERCY?
Gladiators usually fought to the death, but a wounded gladiator could appeal for mercy. The excited crowd would look for the emperor's signal. A thumbs-up meant his life was spared. A thumbs-down meant he must die.

COME ON YOU REDS!

Charioteers belonged to teams and wore their team's colors when they raced. Some also wore protective leather helmets, like the one in this mosaic. In Rome, there were four teams—the Reds, Blues, Whites and Greens. Each team had faithful fans, and charioteers were every bit as popular as football stars are today.

A DAY AT THE RACES

This terra-cotta carving records an exciting moment at the races. Chariot racing was a passion for most Romans. Chariots were usually pulled by four horses, though just two or as many as six could be used. Accidents and foul play were common as the chariots thundered around the track.

THE CHAMP

Boxing was a deadly sport. Fighters, like this boxer, wore studded thongs instead of padded boxing gloves. Severe injuries, and even brain damage, were probably quite common.

THE GREEK IDEAL

The Romans admired all things Greek, including their love of athletics. This painted Greek vase dates from about 333BC and shows long-distance runners. However, Roman crowds were not interested in athletic contests in the Greek style, such as the Olympic Games.

Music and Drama

MUSIC AND SONGS were an important part of Roman life. Music was played at banquets, at weddings and funerals, at the theater, in the home and at fights between gladiators and other public events. The Romans played a variety of musical instruments, including double flutes, panpipes, lyres, cymbals, rattles and tambourines. These had already been well known in either Egypt or Greece. The Romans also had trumpets and horns, and water-powered organs.

Going to the theater was a popular Roman pastime. The whole idea of drama came from Greece, so Greek comedies and tragedies were often performed. Roman writers produced plays in a similar style, as well as comic sketches and dances. The stage used the stone front of a building as a backdrop. Rising banks of stone or wooden seats curved around it in a half circle.

MUSIC LESSONS
Girls from wealthy families often had music lessons at home. This wall painting shows a girl being taught to play the *cithara*, a type of lyre. The Romans adopted this harp-like instrument from the Greeks.

THE ENTERTAINERS
This mosaic from Pompeii shows a group of actors in a scene from a Greek play. Actors were always men, playing the parts of women whenever necessary. The role of actors in a play was shown by the colors of their costume and their masks. The piper in this mosaic is wearing the white mask of a female character.

MAKE A MASK

You will need: self-drying clay, work board, rolling pin, large bowl, modeling knife, acrylic paints, paintbrush, water bowl, scissors, cord, pencil, green paper or cardboard, gardening wire, some colored beads.

1 Put the clay on the board. Roll it out into a sheet that is bigger than the large bowl you are using. Drape it over the bowl and shape it, as shown above.

2 Trim off the edges and cut out eye holes and a mouth. Roll out the clay you trimmed off and cut out a mouth and nose piece, as shown above. Make a small ball of clay, too.

3 Mold the nose onto the mask. Press the small ball of clay into the chin and put the mouth piece over it, as shown. Make a hole on each side of the mask, for the cord.

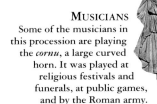

MUSICIANS
Some of the musicians in this procession are playing the *cornu*, a large curved horn. It was played at religious festivals and funerals, at public games, and by the Roman army.

ACTORS' MASKS
Roman actors wore masks and wigs to show the type of character they were playing. This detail of a mosaic from Rome shows the kind of elaborate masks they wore.

DRAMA IN THE OPEN AIR
Roman theaters were usually open to the sky. These are the ruins of the larger of the two theaters in Pompeii. It could seat up to 50,000 people. It had no roof, but could be covered by an awning to protect the audience from the hot summer sun.

4 When the clay is dry, paint the mask in bright colors. You can paint it like this one, shown above, or you could make up your own design. Let the paint dry.

5 Cut two lengths of cord. Thread them through the holes in the sides of the mask, as shown. Secure with a knot. Tie the cord around your head when you wear the mask.

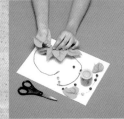

6 Draw, cut out and paint leaf shapes. Thread them onto a length of wire, as shown. Thread beads between some of the leaves. Wind the wire around the top of the mask.

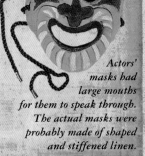

Actors' masks had large mouths for them to speak through. The actual masks were probably made of shaped and stiffened linen.

Fun and Games

ROMAN CHILDREN played games such as hide-and-seek, marbles and hopscotch, which are still popular today. Young children played with dolls and little figures of people and animals. These were made of wood, clay or bronze. A child from a wealthy family might be given a child-size chariot, to be pulled along by a goat.

Roman men and women loved playing board games. There were simple games, similar to tic-tac-toe, and more complicated games, a lot like chess or checkers. In some games, players had to race toward the finish. Dice were thrown to decide how many squares they could move at a time. They played with markers made of bone, glass or clay.

The Romans were great gamblers. They would place bets on a chariot race or a cockfight or on throwing dice. Gambling became such a problem that games of chance were officially banned—except during the winter festival of Saturnalia, when most rules were relaxed. However, the rattle of dice could still be heard in most taverns and public baths.

PLAYING KNUCKLEBONES
Two women play the popular game of knucklebones, or *astragali*. The idea was to throw the knucklebones in the air and catch as many of them as possible on the back of your hand. The number you caught was your score.

KNUCKLEBONES
Most Romans used the ankle bones of sheep to play knucklebones. These had six sides and were also used as dice—each side had a different value. Wealthy Romans might use knucklebones made of glass, bronze or onyx, like these.

MARBLES
Roman children played with these marbles many centuries ago. Two are glass and one is made of pottery. Marbles were either rolled together or onto marked game-boards. They were also thrown into pottery vases. Nuts, such as hazelnuts and walnuts, were often used like marbles.

MAKE A ROMAN GAME
You will need: self-drying clay, rolling pin, cutting board, modeling knife, ruler, glass tiles for making mosaics, two beads (in the same colors as your tiles).

1 Roll out the clay and trim it to about 10 in square. Use the ruler and knife to mark out a grid, 8 squares across and down, leaving a border around the edge.

2 Decorate the border using the clay you trimmed off, as shown above. Let dry. Each player chooses a color and has 16 tiles and a bead—this is the *dux* or leader.

3 Players take turns putting their tiles on any squares, two at a time. The *dux* is put on last. Players now take turns moving a tile one square forward, backward or sideways.

JUST ROLLING ALONG

Children from poor families had few toys and had to work from a young age. However, even poor children found time to play, and made do with whatever was at hand. This boy is rolling wheels in front of him as he runs.

YOUR THROW!

This mosaic from Roman North Africa shows three men playing dice games in a tavern. The Romans loved to gamble and would bet on anything, including the roll of the dice. Large amounts could be won or lost when the dice stopped rolling.

MARKERS

These gaming markers are made of bone and ivory. As well as using quite plain, round ones, the Romans liked to use markers carved in intricate shapes. Here you can see a ram's head, a hare and a lobster. The large round marker has two women carved on it.

DICE

Dice games were played by the poor and the rich. These dice have survived over the centuries. The largest is made of greenstone, the next is made of rock crystal, and the smallest is agate. The silver dice in the form of squatting figures were probably used by wealthy Romans.

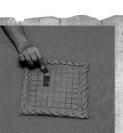

During the game, you must move a tile or dux *if it is possible to do so—even if it means being captured. The winner is the first player to capture all of the other player's tiles and* dux.

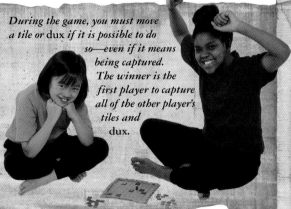

4 If you sandwich your opponent's tile between two of yours, it is captured and removed. You then get an extra turn. The *dux* is captured in the same way as any tile.

5 The *dux* can also jump over a tile to an empty square, as shown. If your opponent's tile is then trapped between your *dux* and one of your tiles, it is captured.

Religions and Festivals

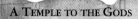

T HE ROMANS believed in many different gods and goddesses. Some of them were the same as the gods of ancient Greece, but with different names. Jupiter, the sky god, was the most powerful of all. Venus was the goddess of love, Mars was the god of war, Ceres the god of the harvest, Saturn the god of farmers, and Mercury of merchants. Household gods protected the home.

Splendid temples were built in honor of the gods. The Pantheon, in Rome, is the largest and most famous. Special festivals for the gods were held during the year, with processions, music, offerings and animal sacrifices. The festivals were often public holidays. The mid-winter festival of Saturnalia, in honor of Saturn, lasted up to seven days.

As the Empire grew, many Romans adopted the religions of other peoples, such as the Egyptians and the Persians.

JUPITER
Jupiter was the chief god of the Romans. He was the all-powerful god of the sky. The Romans believed he showed his anger by hurling a thunderbolt to the ground.

THE PANTHEON
The Pantheon in Rome was a temple to all the gods. It was built between AD118 and 128. Its mosaic floor, interior columns and high dome still remain exactly as they were built.

DIANA THE HUNTRESS
Diana was the goddess of hunting and the Moon. In this detail from a floor mosaic, she is shown poised with a bow and arrow, ready for the hunt. Roman gods were often the same as the Greek ones, but were given different names. Diana's Greek name was Artemis.

A TEMPLE TO THE GODS

You will need: thick stiff cardboard, thin cardboard, old newspaper, scissors, balloon, white glue, ruler, pencils, masking tape, drinking straws, acrylic paints, paintbrush, water bowl, plasticine.

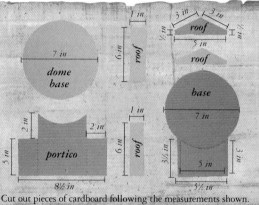

dome base — 7 in — 6 in
roof — 1 in
roof — 3 in / 3 in — ½ in / 5 in / ½ in
roof
base — 7 in

portico — 5 in / 8½ in — 2 in / 2 in
roof — 1 in / 6 in
— 3¾ in / 5 in / 3 in — 5½ in

Cut out pieces of cardboard following the measurements shown.

1 Blow up the balloon. Cover it in strips of newspaper pasted on with glue. Keep pasting until you have a thick layer. Leave to dry. Then burst the balloon and cut out a dome.

PRIESTS OF ISIS

The Egyptian mother-goddess Isis had many followers throughout the Roman Empire. This painting shows priests and worshippers of Isis taking part in a water purification ceremony. The ceremony would have been performed every afternoon.

BLESS THIS HOUSE

This is a bronze statue of a *lar* or household god. Originally gods of the countryside, the *lares* were believed to look after the family and the home. Every Roman home had a shrine to the *lares*. The family, including the children, would make daily offerings to the gods.

MITHRAS THE BULL-SLAYER

Mithras was the Persian god of light. He is shown here, in a marble relief from a temple, slaying a bull. This bull's blood was believed to have brought life to the earth. The cult of Mithras spread through the whole Empire, and was particularly popular with Roman soldiers. However, only men were allowed to worship Mithras.

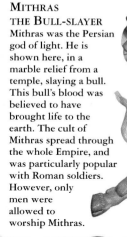

The Pantheon was built of brick and then covered in stone and marble. Its huge dome, with a diameter of over 43 yards, was the largest ever constructed until the 1900s.

2 Put the dome on its card base and draw its outline. Cut out the center of the base to make a halo shape. Make a hole in the top of the dome. Bind the pieces together, as shown.

3 Glue together the base pieces. Cut a piece of thin cardboard long enough to go around the base circle. This will be the circular wall. Use tape to hold the portico in shape.

4 Cut some straws into eight pieces, each 2 in long. These will be the columns for the entrance colonnade. Glue together the roof for the entrance. Secure with tape.

5 Glue together the larger pieces, as shown. Position each straw column with a small piece of plasticine at its base. Glue on the entrance roof. Paint your model.

Family Occasions

THE FAMILY was very important to Romans. The father was the all-powerful head of the family, which included everyone in the household—wife, children, slaves and even close relatives. In the early days of Rome, a father had the power of life and death over his children. However, Roman fathers were rarely harsh and children were much loved by both parents.

Childhood was fairly short. Parents would arrange for a girl to be betrothed at the age of 12, and a boy at 14. Marriages took place a few years later. Brides usually wore a white dress and a yellow cloak, with an orange veil and a wreath of sweetly scented flowers. A sacrifice would be made to the gods, and everyone would wish the couple well. That evening, a procession with flaming torches and flute music would lead the newlyweds to their home.

Funerals also featured music and processions. By Roman law, burials and cremations had to take place outside the city walls.

HAPPY FAMILIES
This Roman tombstone from Germany shows a family gathered together for a meal. From the Latin inscription on it, we know that it was put up by a soldier of the legions, in memory of his dead wife. He lovingly describes her as the "sweetest and purest" of women.

MOTHER AND BABY
A mother tenderly places her baby in the cradle. When children were born, they were laid at the feet of their father. If he accepted the child into the family, he would pick it up. In wealthy families, a birth was a great joy, but for poorer families it just meant another mouth to feed. Romans named a girl on the 8th day after the birth, and a boy on the 9th day. The child was given a *bulla*, a charm to ward off evil spirits.

TOGETHERNESS
When a couple became engaged, they would exchange gifts as a symbol of their devotion to each other. A ring like this one might have been given by a man to his future bride. The clasped hands symbolize marriage. Gold pendants with similar patterns were also popular.

MOURNING THE DEAD

A wealthy Roman has died and his family has gone into mourning. Laments are played on flutes as they prepare his body for the funeral procession. The Romans believed that the dead went to Hades, the Underworld, which lay beyond the river of the dead. A coin was placed in the corpse's mouth, to pay the ferryman. Food and drink for the journey were buried with the body.

TILL DEATH US DO PART

A Roman marriage ceremony was a lot like a present-day Christian wedding. The couple would exchange vows and clasp hands to symbolize their union. Here, the groom is holding the marriage contract, which would have been drawn up before the ceremony. Not everyone found happiness, however, and divorce was quite common.

WEDDING FLOWERS

Roman brides wore a veil on their wedding day. This was often crowned with a wreath of flowers. In the early days of the Empire, verbena and sweet marjoram were a popular combination. Later fashions included orange blossom and myrtle, whose fragrant flowers were sacred to Venus, the goddess of love.

orange blossom

verbena

Soldiers of the Legions

THE ARMY OF THE EARLY EMPIRE was divided into 28 groups called legions. Each of these numbered about 5,500 soldiers. The legion included mounted troops and foot-soldiers. They were organized into cohorts of about 500 men, and centuries of about 80 men—even though centuries means "hundreds." Each legion was led into battle by soldiers carrying standards. These were decorated poles that represented the honor and bravery of the legion.

The first Roman soldiers were called up from the wealthier families in times of war. These conscripts had to supply their own weapons. In later years, the Roman army became paid professionals, with legionaries recruited from all citizens. During the period of the Empire, many foreign troops also fought for Rome as auxiliary soldiers.

Army life was tough and discipline was severe. After a long march carrying heavy kits, tents, tools and weapons, the weary soldiers would have to dig camp defenses. A sentry who deserted his post would be beaten to death.

AT WAR
Trajan's Column in Rome is decorated with scenes from the Dacian wars. These were fought in the region of present-day Romania. Scenes like these can tell us much about Roman soldiers, the weapons they used, their enemies and their allies.

A LEGIONARY
This bronze statue of a legionary is about 1,800 years old. He is wearing a crested parade helmet and the overlapping bronze armor of the period. Legionaries underwent strict training and were brutally disciplined. They were tough soldiers and quite a force to be reckoned with.

ON HORSEBACK
Roman foot-soldiers were backed up by mounted troops, or cavalry. They were divided into groups of 500 to 1,000, called *alae*. The cavalry were among the highest paid of Roman soldiers.

RAISING THE STANDARD

The Emperor Constantine addresses his troops, probably congratulating them on a victory. They are carrying standards, emblems of each legion. Standards were decorated with gold eagles, hands, wreaths and banners called *vexilla*. They were symbols of the honor and bravery of the legion and had to be protected at all costs.

A ROMAN FORT

The Roman army built forts of wood or stone all over the Empire. This fort is in southern Britain. It was built to defend the coast against attacks by Saxon raiders from northern Europe. Today, its surrounding area is called Porchester. The name comes from a combination of the word port and *caster*, the Latin word for fort.

HADRIAN'S WALL

This is part of Hadrian's Wall, which marks the most northerly border of the Roman Empire. It stretches for 75 miles across northern England, almost from coast to coast. It was built as a defensive barrier between AD122 and 128, at the command of the Emperor Hadrian.

Weapons and Armor

ROMAN SOLDIERS were well equipped. A legionary was armed with a dagger, called a *pugio*, and a short iron sword, called a *gladius*, which was used for stabbing and slashing. He carried a javelin, or *pilum*, made of iron and wood. In the early days, a foot-soldier's armor was a mail shirt, worn over a short, thick tunic. Officers wore a cuirass, a bronze casing that protected the chest and back. By about AD35, the mail shirt was being replaced by plate armor made of iron. The metal sections were joined by hooks or by leather straps. Officers wore varying crests to show their rank. Early shields were oval, and later ones were oblong with curved edges. They were made of layers of wood glued together, covered in leather and linen. A metal boss, or cover, over the central handle could be used to hit an enemy who got too close.

ROMAN SOLDIERS
Artists over the ages have been inspired by the battles of the Roman legions. They imagined how fully armed Roman soldiers might have looked. This picture shows a young officer giving orders.

HEAD GEAR
Helmets were designed to protect the sides of the head and the neck. This cavalry helmet is made of bronze and iron. It would have been worn by an auxiliary, a foreign soldier fighting for Rome sometime after AD43. Officers wore crests on their helmets, so that their men could see them during battle.

ROMAN ARMOR

You will need: tape measure, sheets of silver cardboard (one or two, depending on how big you are), scissors, pencil, white glue, paintbrush, 2 yards length of cord, compass.

1 Measure yourself around your chest. Cut out three strips of cardboard, 2 in wide and long enough to go around you. Cut out thin strips to stick these three together.

2 Lay the wide strips flat and glue them together with the thin strips, as shown above. The Romans would have used leather straps to hold the wide metal pieces together.

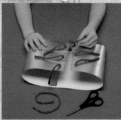

3 When the glue is dry, bend the ends together, silver side out. Make a hole in the end of each strip and thread the cord through, as shown above.

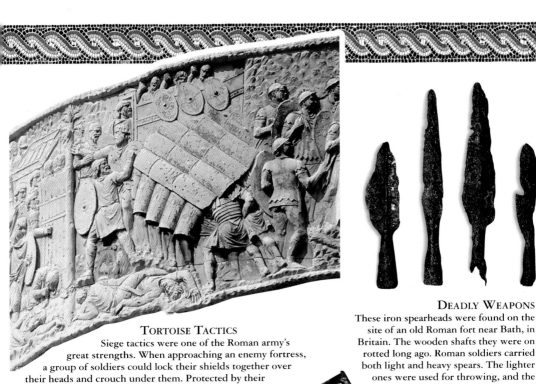

TORTOISE TACTICS

Siege tactics were one of the Roman army's great strengths. When approaching an enemy fortress, a group of soldiers could lock their shields together over their heads and crouch under them. Protected by their shields, they could safely advance toward the enemy. This was known as the tortoise, or *testudo,* formation. During a siege, catapults were used to hurl iron bolts and large stones over fortress walls.

DEADLY WEAPONS

These iron spearheads were found on the site of an old Roman fort near Bath, in Britain. The wooden shafts they were on rotted long ago. Roman soldiers carried both light and heavy spears. The lighter ones were used for throwing, and the heavier ones were for thrusting at close range.

SWORDS

Both short and long swords would have been kept in a scabbard. This spectacular scabbard was owned by an officer who served the Emperor Tiberius. It may have been given to him by the Emperor himself. It is elaborately decorated in gold and silver.

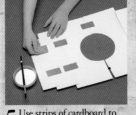

4 Cut a square of cardboard as wide as your shoulders. Use the compass to draw a 3-in diameter circle in the center. Cut the square in half and cut out the half circles.

5 Use strips of cardboard to glue the shoulder halves together, leaving a neck hole. Cut out four more strips, two a little shorter than the others. Attach them in the same way.

Put the shoulder piece over your head and tie the chest section around yourself. Now you are a legionary ready to do battle with the enemies of Rome. Metal strip armor was invented during the reign of the Emperor Tiberius, AD14-37. *Originally, the various parts were hinged and were joined either by hooks or by buckles and straps.*

Ships and Sailors

THE ROMANS USED SHIPS for trade, transport and warfare. Roman warships were slim, fast vessels called galleys. They were powered by oarsmen who sat below deck. A standard Roman war galley had 270 oarsmen. It also had a large, square sail that was used for more speed when the wind was favorable.

All kinds of goods, from wool and pottery to marble and grain, had to be moved around the Empire. Most goods, especially heavy cargoes of food or building materials, were moved by water. Merchant ships were deeper, heavier and slower than galleys. They had big, flapping sails and longer oars to make steering easier. Barges were used on rivers.

The Romans built lighthouses on treacherous coasts—stone towers topped by big lanterns or blazing beacons. Pirates, uncharted waters and the weather also made sea travel dangerous.

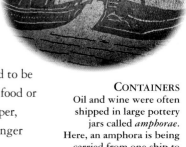

CONTAINERS
Oil and wine were often shipped in large pottery jars called *amphorae*. Here, an amphora is being carried from one ship to another. The amphorae were usually stacked in the ship's hold, with layers of brushwood as padding.

AT THE DOCKS
This wall painting from the port of Ostia shows a merchant ship being loaded. Heavy sacks of grain are being carried on board. You can see the two large steering oars at the stern, or rear, of the ship.

ROLLING ON THE RIVER
Wine and other liquids were sometimes stored in barrels. These were transported by river barges, like the one in this carving. Barrels of wine would be hauled from the vineyards of Germany or southern France to the nearest seaport.

MAKE AN AMPHORA

You will need: sheet of thin cardboard, ruler, two pencils, scissors, corrugated cardboard—two circles of 4 in and 8 in in diameter, two strips of 16 in x 12 in and another large piece, masking tape, white glue, old newspaper, paintbrush, reddish-brown acrylic paint, water bowl.

1 Cut two pieces of cardboard— 2 in and 15 in in depth. Tape the short piece to the circle. Curl the long piece to make the neck. Make two holes in the side and tape it to the large circle.

2 Roll up the strips of corrugated cardboard. Bend them, as shown, attaching one end to the hole in the neck and the other to the cardboard. Set in place with glue and tape.

3 Cut a piece of cardboard, 6 square in. Roll it into a cylinder shape. Cut four lines, 4 in long, at one end, so it can be tapered into a point, as shown. Bind with tape.

SAILING OFF TO BATTLE

This painting imagines the impressive spectacle of a Roman war galley leaving harbor on its way to battle. Galleys were powered by rows of oarsmen, who sat on benches below deck. The helmsman, who controlled the galley's steering, shouted orders down to them. This galley has three banks, or layers, of oars. An underwater battering ram stuck out from the bow, or front, of war galleys. During a sea battle, the mast was lowered and the galley would try to ram the enemy ship. With the ram stuck in its side, Roman soldiers could easily board the enemy ship to finish the fight man to man.

An amphora like this one might have been used to carry wine, oil or fish sauce. Its long, pointed end would be stuck into layers of brushwood for support during transport.

4 To give the amphora a more solid base, roll up a cone of corrugated cardboard and stick it around the tapered end. Push a pencil into the end, as shown. Tape in position.

5 Stick the neck onto the main body. Cover the whole piece with strips of newspaper brushed on with glue. Let dry. Repeat until you have built up a thick layer.

6 When the paper is dry, paint the amphora. Roman amphorae were made of clay, so use a reddish-brown paint to make yours look like it is clay. Let dry.

Builders of the Empire

THE ROMANS were great builders and engineers. As the legions conquered foreign lands, they built new roads to carry their supplies and messengers. The roads were very straight, stretching across hundreds of miles. They were built with a slight hump in the middle so that rainwater drained off to the sides. Some were paved with stone and others were covered with gravel or stone chippings. Roman engineers also used their skills to bring water supplies to their cities by building aqueducts.

The Romans constructed great domes, arched bridges and grand public buildings all across the Empire. Local supplies of stone and timber were used. Stone was an important Roman building material, but had to be quarried and transported to sites. The Romans were the first to develop concrete, which was cheaper and stronger than stone.

The rule of the Romans came to an end in western Europe over 1,500 years ago. Yet reminders of their skills and organization are still visible today.

ROMAN ROADS
A typical Roman road, stretching into the distance as far as the eye can see. It runs through the coastal town of Ostia, in Italy. It was the 1800s before anyone in Europe could build roads to match those of ancient Rome.

MUSCLE POWER
This stone carving shows how Romans used big wooden cranes to lift heavy building materials. The crane is powered by a huge treadwheel. Slaves walk around and around in the wheel, making it turn. The turning wheel pulls on the rope, which is tied around the heavy block of stone, raising it off the ground.

MAKE A GROMA

You will need: large piece of cardboard, scissors, ruler, pencil, square of cardboard, white glue, masking tape, balsa wood pole, plasticine, silver foil, string, large sewing needle, acrylic paints, paintbrush, water bowl, broom handle.

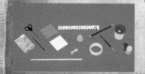

1 Cut out three pieces of cardboard—two 8 in x 2½ in, one 16 in x 2½ in. Cut another piece, 6 in x 5 in, for the handle. Then cut them into shape, as shown above.

2 Measure to the center of the long piece. Use a pencil to make a slot here, between the layers of cardboard. The slot is for the balsa wood pole.

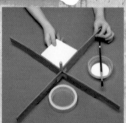

3 Slide the pole into the slot and tape the cardboard pieces in a cross. Use the cardboard square to make sure the four arms of the groma are at right angles. Glue in place.

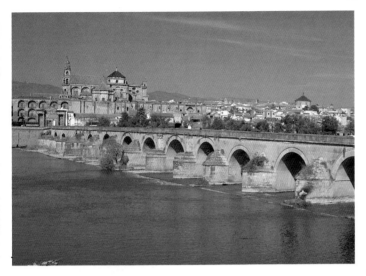

The Romans used a variety of stones for building. Local quarries were the most common source. Limestone and a volcanic rock called tufa were used in Pompeii. Slate was used for roofing in parts of Britain. Fine marble, used for temples and other public buildings, was available in the Carrara region of Italy, as it still is today. However, it was also imported from overseas.

marble

slate

SURVIVING THE CENTURIES
This Roman bridge crosses the River Guadalquivir at Córdoba in Spain. The Romans had no bulldozers or power tools, and yet their buildings and monuments have survived thousands of years.

WALLS OF ROME
The city of Rome's defenses were built at many stages throughout its history. These walls were raised during the reign of the Emperor Marcus Aurelius, AD121–180. Known as the Aurelian Walls, they are still in good condition today.

Slot the arms onto the balsa wood pole. Use the plumb lines as a guide to make sure the pole is vertical. The arms can then be used to line up objects in the distance. Romans used a groma to measure right angles and to make sure roads were straight.

4 Roll the plasticine into four small cones and cover them with foil. Thread string through the tops, as shown. These are the groma's plumb lines, or vertical guides.

5 Tie the plumb lines to each arm, as shown. They must all hang at the same length—8 in will do. If the plasticine is too heavy, use wet newspaper rolled up in the foil.

6 Split the top of the handle piece, and wrap it around the balsa wood pole. Glue it in place, as shown. Do the same on the other end with the broom handle. Paint the groma.

Glossary

A

amphitheater An oval, open-air arena surrounded by seats. It was invented by the Romans for public shows such as gladiators fighting to the death and battles between wild animals.

amphora (plural: amphorae) A pottery storage jar, often shaped like a tall vase with handles and a pointed base. Amphorae came in all shapes and sizes—tall and slim, fat and round.

anvil A block used by smiths for shaping hot metals.

aqueduct

aqueduct An artificial channel for carrying water over a long distance. Aqueducts were usually underground or were supported on arched bridges.

arena The dirt floor area in an amphitheater where games and combats took place.

atrium The hallway or courtyard in a Roman house. The center of the atrium was open to the sky.

auxiliaries Soldiers recruited from non-Roman citizens.

B

basilica A building in the forum of a Roman city, used as law courts and a town hall.

blacksmith A craftsman who makes or repairs iron goods.

brazier A bronze container filled with hot coals, used for heating rooms.

C

catapult A large wooden structure used during a siege to fire stones and iron bolts at the enemy.

chariot

century A unit of the Roman army, numbering from 80 to 100 soldiers.

chariot A lightweight cart drawn by horses. Chariots were used in warfare or for racing.

circus An oval track used for chariot races.

citizen A free person with the right to vote.

civilization A society that has made advances in the arts, science and technology, law or government.

cohort A division of the Roman army, at times numbering about 500 soldiers.

conscript Someone who is called up by the government to serve in the army.

consul One of the two leaders of the Roman republic, elected each year.

cremation The burning of dead bodies.

cuirass Armor that protects the upper part of the body.

curia The council in ancient Roman cities.

Consul

D

dictator A ruler with total power.

E

emperor The ruler of an empire.

empire A large number of different lands ruled over by a single person or government.

estate A large amount of land, houses and farms, usually owned by a single person or group.

F

flax A plant whose stems are used to make a cloth called linen. Its blue flowers can be used to make a dye, and its seeds are crushed to produce linseed oil.

forceps Surgical instruments shaped like pincers or tongs.

forum The town center or downtown area of a Roman city.

G

galley A warship powered by oars.

gladiator A professional fighter, a slave or a criminal who fought to the death for public entertainment.

graffiti Words or pictures scrawled or scratched in public places, particularly on walls.

grid pattern A criss-cross pattern of straight lines at right angles. It was used to divide a town into blocks and straight streets.

groma An instrument used by Roman surveyors. They used it to measure right angles and to make sure roads were straight.

gruel A soup of cereal and water, such as porridge.

guild A society that protected the interests of people working within a trade.

J

javelin A throwing spear.

K

kiln An industrial oven, or a furnace.

kindling Twigs, woodchips or other material used to start a fire.

L

legion A section of the Roman army made up only

legionary

of Roman Citizens. Non-Roman citizens could not be legionaries.

litter A form of transport in which a seat or platform is carried by bearers.

lyre One of various harp-like instruments played in ancient Greece and Rome.

M

mail Chain armor, made up of interlocking iron rings.

midwife Someone who helps a woman to give birth.

mosaic

mosaic A picture made up from many small squares or cubes of glass, stone or pottery, set in soft concrete.

myrrh A kind of resin from shrubs, used to make perfume and medicine.

O

ocher An earthy iron ore used as pigment. It is usually red or yellow.

P

palla A large shawl that could be arranged in various ways.

panpipes A musical instrument made up of a series of pipes of different lengths.

papyrus A reed that grows on the River Nile. It is used to make a kind of paper.

patrician A member of one of the old, wealthy and powerful families in ancient Rome.

plate armor Fitted body armor made of linked sheets of solid metal.

plebeian A member of the (free) common people of ancient Rome.

preserve To treat food so that it does not spoil or go bad.

R

ram A large, pointed beam extending from the hull, or front, of an ancient warship. It was used to ram into the side of an enemy ship, making it easeir to board.

republic A state that is governed by an assembly of its citizens rather than by a king.

S

sacrifice The killing of a living thing in honor of the gods.

Samian ware A type of glazed, red-clay pottery that was popular throughout the Roman Empire.

Samian pot

Saturnalia A winter festival held in honor of the god Saturn.

Senate The law-making assembly of ancient Rome.

sickle A tool with a curved blade used to cut grass or grain crops.

society All the classes of people living in a particular community or country.

standard A banner used by armies to rally their troops in battle or carried in parades.

stola A long dress worn by Roman women. It was worn over a tunic.

oil flask and strigils

strigil A metal scraper used for cleaning the body.

stylus A pointed tool, such as the one used to scratch words onto a wax tablet.

survey To map out and measure the land. Land is surveyed before the construction of a building or a road, or any other structure.

T

tablinium The formal reception room and study in a Roman house.

terra-cotta Baked, unglazed, orange-red clay.

toga A white woolen robe, worn by the upper classes in ancient Rome.

tortoise or testudo A method of covering a group of soldiers with shields to protect them from missiles.

treadwheel A wooden wheel turned by the feet of people, used to power mills or other machinery.

tribune One of the officials elected to represent the interests of the common people in ancient Rome. Tribune was also a rank in the Roman army.

triclinium Dining room. Its name comes from the Roman tradition of having an arrangement of three (tri) couches to lie on while dining.

trident

trident A three-pronged spear used by fishermen and gladiators.

trivet A metal stand placed over a flame to support a cooking pot.

tunic A simple, shirt-like garment.

tutor A personal teacher.

V

villa A Roman country house, often decorated with mosaics and wall paintings. Villas were usually part of an argicultural estate.

Index